Learning to Write
Descriptive Paragraphs

Frances Purslow

WEIGL PUBLISHERS INC.

Published by Weigl Publishers Inc.
350 5th Avenue, 59th Floor
New York, NY 10118

Website: www.weigl.com

Library of Congress Cataloging-in-Publication Data

Purslow, Frances.
  Descriptive paragraphs / Frances Purslow.
      p. cm. -- (Learning to write)
  Includes index.
  ISBN 978-1-59036-737-7 (hard cover : alk. paper) -- ISBN 978-1-59036-738-4 (soft cover : alk. paper)
  1. Composition (Language arts)--Juvenile literature. 2. English language--Paragraphs--Juvenile literature.
  3. Description (Rhetoric)--Juvenile literature. I. Title.
  LB1576.P875 2008
  372.62'3--dc22
                        2007012723

Printed in the United States in North Mankato, Minnesota
2 3 4 5 6 7 8 9 0 14 13 12 11 10

042010
WEP060410

Editor: Heather C. Hudak
Design: Terry Paulhus

Table of Contents

Learning about Descriptive Paragraphs

A descriptive paragraph is a group of sentences that describes a noun. A noun is a person, a place, or a thing. A descriptive paragraph may be complete by itself, or it may be part of a longer piece of writing, such as a story.

The following is an example of a descriptive paragraph. This paragraph describes Abraham Lincoln.

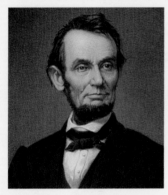

As a child, Abraham Lincoln was known to be a good storyteller and to have a keen sense of humor. Later, Lincoln was a skilled lawyer and a respected member of the Republican party. He had excellent debate skills and was hard working. Lincoln became the sixteenth president of the United States in 1860. He had firm beliefs about slavery, which led to the **Emancipation Proclamation.** *Lincoln is considered one of the greatest presidents of all time.*

In this picture, Lincoln is riding a horse past his house in Springfield, Illinois. He had just won the presidential campaign against Senator Stephen Douglas.

How would you describe Lincoln's house as it is shown in this picture? Visit **www.nps.gov/liho** to learn more about Lincoln's house. Make a list of the describing words used on the website.

Using Words to Describe People, Places, and Things

Look at the pictures, and read the text beside each one. The text is a description of the American site, symbol, or president shown in the picture.

Person

*John F. Kennedy was the 35th president of the United States. He was the youngest person to be **elected** as president. Kennedy was a Democrat. He believed in the **Civil Rights Movement**. Kennedy was a popular leader. He spoke well, and many young people looked up to him.*

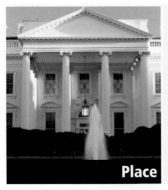

Place

The White House is located on Pennsylvania Avenue in Washington, DC. It is a large, white building with columns. The White House has two wings, the East Wing and the West Wing. Each wing is three stories high. In the center is the main building. The White House has many green lawns and lush gardens.

Thing

The national flag is one of the best-known symbols of the United States. It is often called the Star-Spangled Banner because of its stars and stripes. The stripes represent the original 13 colonies of the United States. The stars symbolize each of the country's 50 states.

What words can be used to describe the people, places, and things you see in these pictures? For example, by looking at the picture of the flag, you can tell that it has 13 horizontal stripes that alternate red and white. A blue rectangle in the upper left corner features 50 white stars.

What are Adjectives?

In the description of Abraham Lincoln, you learned that he had excellent debate skills. The words "excellent" and "debate" describe his skills.

To write a descriptive paragraph, you will need many describing words. Describing words are called adjectives. Adjectives describe nouns. For example, look at the following painting, and read the descriptive paragraph.

George Washington was a strong, powerful leader. He was a very wealthy landowner. Washington was the Commander in Chief of the Continental Army in the **American Revolution***. He was a well-respected military leader. In 1781, Washington played an important role in the siege of Yorktown. Later, Washington became the first president of the United States. Many felt he was an honorable and impressive man.*

The words "strong" and "powerful" are adjectives. They describe the noun "leader." They tell us what kind of leader George Washington was. Find three other adjectives in the descriptive paragraph above. Looking at the image, how can you tell which person is George Washington? Use five adjectives to describe what he looks like.

Learning to Use Adjectives

Use adjectives to describe your state flag or one of the state flags on this page.

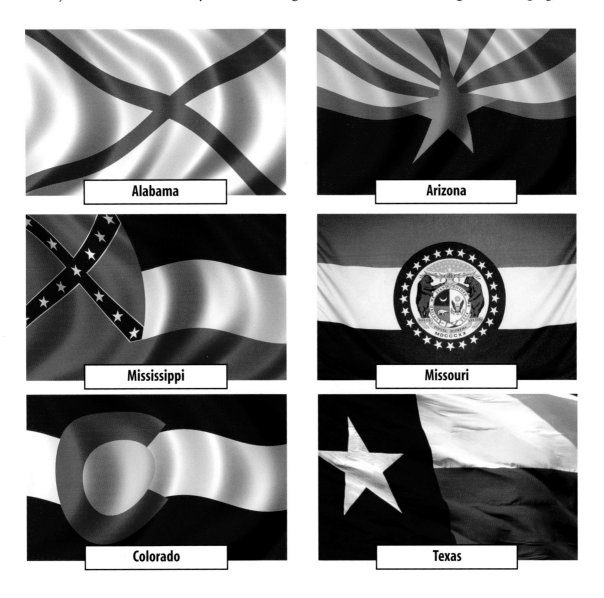

Alabama

Arizona

Mississippi

Missouri

Colorado

Texas

Words such as "red," "rectangular," and "striped" are adjectives. However, there are many other words that have a similar meaning. For example, instead of using the word "red" to describe your flag, you could use "crimson" or "scarlet." When writing the descriptive paragraph about your flag, use a thesaurus to find alternate words to describe the colors, shapes, and images.

Using the Senses

Not all descriptive paragraphs describe how something looks. Some describe how something feels to touch. Others describe how something tastes, sounds, or smells. Sometimes a paragraph will include a description using many senses.

Read the following description of the bald eagle. Note that two senses are used in the paragraph. The bald eagle's feathers are described as soft and brown. This tells you how the feathers look and how they feel. As you read, find other descriptions of how the eagle looks and how it feels to touch.

In 1782, the Founding Fathers named the bald eagle the national bird of the United States. The eagle is a large, powerful bird that represents strength, freedom, courage, and **immortality**. *A bald eagle has soft, brown feathers on most of its body and white feathers on its head and tail. It has a bony eyebrow ridge that gives it a* **fierce** *appearance. Bald eagles have long, razor-sharp talons, or claws, and spiky knobs on their toes.*

Look at the picture of the bald eagle. Using the senses of sight and touch, think about how you would describe the look and feel of the eagle. You might say that the eagle's feathers are silky and downy. What other words would you use to describe the eagle's feathers, eyes, feet, and beak?

Using Your Senses to Describe Thanksgiving

Read the paragraph about Thanksgiving to learn how it was first celebrated.

The pilgrims and the Wampanoag Indians celebrated the first special days of thanksgiving nearly 400 years ago. Today, Thanksgiving Day is one of the most important family celebrations in the United States. It is a national holiday. Held on the fourth Thursday of November, Thanksgiving Day is a distinct time to give thanks for close family and friends, warm shelter, plentiful food, and good health. Golden brown turkey, piping-hot potatoes, and sweet cranberry sauce are some of the main dishes served on Thanksgiving Day.

Americans celebrate Thanksgiving Day with family and friends. Many people enjoy a large afternoon meal. The meal often includes corn, turkey, cranberries, and pumpkin pie. The main dish is often a big, stuffed turkey. Use adjectives to describe the taste of some of the Thanksgiving Day foods in these pictures. For example, you might write "buttery corn."

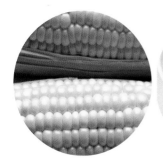

Parts of a Descriptive Paragraph

A descriptive paragraph has three parts. The first part is the topic sentence. The topic sentence is usually the first sentence. It tells readers what the paragraph will be about and catches their attention. Supporting sentences generally follow the topic sentence. They provide details explaining or supporting the topic sentence.

At the end of a descriptive paragraph, a sentence wraps up, or summarizes, the ideas expressed in the paragraph. This is called the concluding sentence. It is usually a strong statement.

Independence Day is a special birthday party for the United States. **It is an incredible event that is celebrated on the Fourth of July. On this day, excited Americans hold patriotic celebrations with colorful fireworks and festive music. They have delicious picnics and watch fun parades. Most importantly, on the Fourth of July, Americans celebrate their independence and freedom.**

The topic sentence is shown in red in the paragraph about Independence Day. Can you tell which are the supporting and concluding sentences?

Identifying the Parts

Look at the photo, and write a topic sentence about an Independence Day celebration. Then, write two or three supporting sentences describing when and how the holiday is celebrated. Finally, write a strong, concluding sentence.

Describing a Favorite Holiday

Read the following examples of descriptive paragraphs about U.S. holidays. Then, think about your favorite holiday. Research the origins and traditions of that holiday, and write a descriptive paragraph about it. Remember to state your main idea in a topic sentence. For example, you might write, "My favorite holiday is Presidents' Day." Then, write supporting sentences that add details about the holiday. You might describe the foods you eat and ways you decorate. Finally, end with a concluding sentence that sums up your feelings about the holiday. Be sure to include adjectives to describe nouns, and use your senses to describe how nouns look, taste, smell, sound, or feel to touch.

Each year, Americans celebrate Veterans Day on November 11. On this day, solemn events take place at war memorials across the country. Veterans, soldiers, and citizens place colorful flowers and American flags on graves. Some people quietly pay their respects at private services. At many special ceremonies, a bugler plays Taps. *Veterans may march in a parade. Veterans Day is a tribute to those who serve to protect America's freedom.*

Cinco de Mayo *is a symbol of Mexican strength and unity. It is Spanish for "the fifth of May." Every year on this day, special Cinco de Mayo celebrations take place across Mexico and the United States. Children dress is festive costumes and perform traditional songs and dances. People find many exciting ways to celebrate being Mexican.*

On the third Monday of January each year, Americans celebrate Martin Luther King, Jr. Day. This holiday celebrates the extraordinary work of Dr. King. People march in peaceful parades and attend special church services. Many people volunteer on this day. They spend quality time with seniors, cook delicious meals for the less fortunate, or tutor those who need help.

Ramadan is an important month in the **Muslim** calendar. During this time, Muslims fast. For some, Ramadan includes special activities, such as festivals, prayers, and retreats. It often ends with a big family gathering and large meal. Homes are decorated with colorful flowers and bright lights.

On the second Monday of October, Americans celebrate Columbus Day. On this unique holiday, there are large parades and exciting festivals to honor when Christopher Columbus discovered America. Some celebrations feature Italian-American celebrities and traditional music and dancing. They may include tasty Italian foods, such as crusty bread, olive oil, and prosciutto.

Understanding Unity

All of the sentences in a descriptive paragraph should relate to the same topic. This is called unity. If a paragraph does not have unity, then one or more sentences do not relate to the main idea, as stated in the topic sentence. The following paragraph has unity. All of the sentences are about Independence Hall.

*Independence Hall is the birthplace of the United States. The red brick building is located in Philadelphia, Pennsylvania. Independence Hall was built in the **Georgian style**. This building has many windows. There is a bell tower at the top of the building. Independence Hall is a special building. It was the site of many important historic events in the United States, such as the **adoption** of the Declaration of Independence and the signing of the **Constitution** of the United States.*

Which Sentence Does Not Belong?

The following paragraph does not have unity. It includes a sentence that does not relate to the main topic. Which sentence does not refer to the Statue of Liberty?

The Statue of Liberty is a well-known symbol of freedom. It stands on Liberty Island in New York. The huge statue was a special gift from the people of France to the people of the United States. It honors the strong alliance, or friendship, between France and the United States during the American Revolution. The large statue shows a woman escaping from the chains of **tyranny**. *She wears a crown with seven pointy spikes. New York City is a large city. The spikes represent the seven seas and seven continents. She holds a torch in her right hand and a tablet in her left hand. The date of Independence Day, July 4, 1776, is written on the stone tablet.*

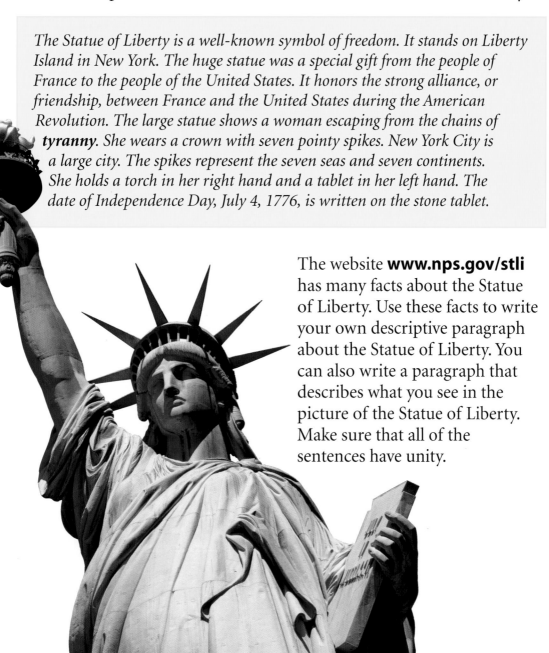

The website **www.nps.gov/stli** has many facts about the Statue of Liberty. Use these facts to write your own descriptive paragraph about the Statue of Liberty. You can also write a paragraph that describes what you see in the picture of the Statue of Liberty. Make sure that all of the sentences have unity.

Creating Coherence

The ideas in a paragraph should flow in a logical order from beginning to end. This is called coherence. Connecting words, such as "then," "next," and "finally," help show the order of time. These connecting words are called transitions. They connect the sentences and show the sequence of events.

Other transitions can be used to describe something in order of place, such as "nearby," "above," "inside," and "at the top."

The following paragraph describes the development of the Presidential Flag and Seal. Notice the transitions that show the order of time.

The design of the Presidential Flag and Seal has changed many times. Both the flag and seal have an eagle clutching arrows in one claw and an olive branch in the other. Before 1945, the eagle's head faced the arrows. Then, President Harry S. Truman changed the direction of the eagle's head. He wanted to focus on peace, not war. Today, the eagle's head faces the olive branch instead of the arrows.

Put These Sentences in Order

This picture is of the U.S. Capitol. The following sentences describe the building and what it is used for. Can you figure out the correct order of the sentences to create a descriptive paragraph with coherence? Look for clues to the correct order.

A. The U.S. Capitol is made mostly of white marble.

B. In the center, the wings are connected by a central section.

C. The main floor structure has a central section and two wings that extend north and south.

D. On top of the dome stands a statue of a woman.

E. Above the central section is a large, circular dome.

Answers: 1. A 2. C 3. B 4. E 5. D

Tools for Paragraph Writing

What did you learn? Look at the questions in the "Skills" column. Compare them to the page number in the "Page" column. Refresh your memory about the content you learned during this part of the paragraph writing process by reading the "Content" column below.

SKILLS	CONTENT		PAGE
Using words to describe		Abraham Lincoln, John F. Kennedy, White House, U.S. flag	4–5
Using adjectives		George Washington	6–7
Knowing how to write using the senses		bald eagle, Thanksgiving	8–9
Understanding the parts of a descriptive paragraph		Independence Day	10–11
Ensuring sentences have unity		Independence Hall, Statue of Liberty	14–15
Making sure the paragraph has coherence		Presidential Flag and Seal, U.S. Capitol	16–17

Practice Writing Different Types of Sentences

Look at the computerized image. It shows many important U.S. symbols.

The large White House is the official residence of the president of the United States. The U.S. Capitol is a beautiful building that is the seat of the U.S. Congress in Washington, DC. The tall Washington Monument is an important national memorial honoring the great George Washington. The marble Lincoln Memorial is a monument dedicated to Abraham Lincoln. All four symbols are located in Washington, DC.

Use the Internet, or visit the library to find out more information about these four American symbols. Then, write a describing sentence about each of the symbols in the image. Try writing one of each of the following types of sentences.

In a telling sentence, the writer tells about something. This sentence ends with a period.

Asking sentences ask questions. They end with a question mark.

An exclaiming sentence shows emotion. It ends with an exclamation point.

Commanding sentences give direct orders. They end with a period.

Put Your Knowledge to Use

Put your knowledge of descriptive paragraphs to use by writing about a U.S. symbol.

Here is a photograph of Mount Rushmore. The paragraph about Mount Rushmore has a topic sentence, supporting sentences, and a concluding sentence. The sentences flow in a logical order and are related to each other. There are many adjectives throughout the text.

*Mount Rushmore is a national monument in South Dakota. It is a massive sculpture in the side of a 5,725-foot-tall mountain. Mount Rushmore consists of granite and **metamorphic** rock. It honors the United States' greatest leaders. It has 60-foot-tall carvings of the faces of four influential U.S. presidents. They are George Washington, Thomas Jefferson, Abraham Lincoln, and Theodore Roosevelt. Mount Rushmore is one of the best-known symbols of America.*

Before you begin your paragraph, choose one of the U.S. symbols from the three pictures on this page. Research information about the symbol you have chosen. Then, make a list of adjectives that describe it. Include many of these adjectives in your descriptive paragraph.

Make sure that your paragraph has a topic sentence, supporting sentences, and a concluding sentence. Choose only sentences that relate to your topic. Finally, be sure that the ideas in your paragraph flow in a logical order from beginning to end.

Washington Monument

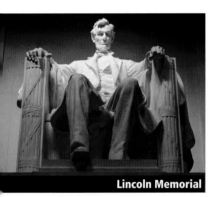
Lincoln Memorial

The Pentagon

EXPANDED CHECKLIST

Reread your paragraph, and make sure that you have all of the following.

- ☑ My paragraph has a topic sentence.
- ☑ My paragraph has supporting sentences.
- ☑ My paragraph has a concluding sentence.
- ☑ All of the sentences in my paragraph relate to the same topic.
- ☑ All of the ideas in my paragraph flow in a logical order.
- ☑ My paragraph has adjectives.

Types of Paragraphs

Now you have learned the tools for writing descriptive paragraphs. You can use your knowledge of adjectives, the senses, parts of a paragraph, unity, and coherence to write descriptive paragraphs. There are three other types of paragraphs. You can use some of the same tools you learned in this book to write all types of paragraphs. The chart below shows other types of paragraphs and their key features.

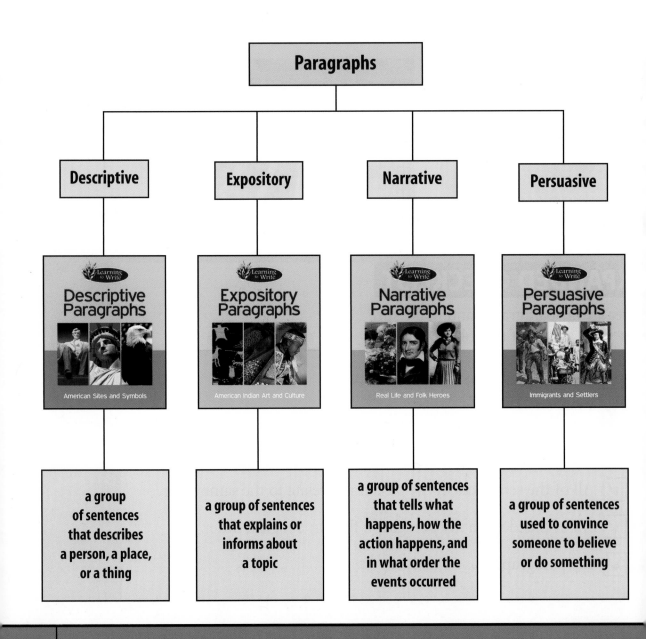

Paragraphs

Descriptive — a group of sentences that describes a person, a place, or a thing

Expository — a group of sentences that explains or informs about a topic

Narrative — a group of sentences that tells what happens, how the action happens, and in what order the events occurred

Persuasive — a group of sentences used to convince someone to believe or do something

Websites for Further Research

Many books and websites provide information on writing descriptive paragraphs. To learn more about writing this type of paragraph, borrow books from the library, or surf the Internet.

To find out more about writing descriptive paragraphs, type key words, such as "writing paragraphs," into the search field of your Web browser. There are many sites that teach about American sites and symbols. You can use these sites to practice writing descriptive paragraphs. Begin by selecting one topic from the site. Read about the topic, and then use the checklist on page 21 to write a paragraph.

Visit *A to Z Kids Stuff* to learn about symbols such as the American Flag, the national anthem, and the Liberty Bell. www.atozkidsstuff.com/symbols.html

Ben's Guide to U.S. Government for Kids provides information about historical documents, branches of government, and government symbols. http://bensguide.gpo.gov/index.html

Glossary

adoption: formal acceptance or approval

American Revolution: the period between 1775 and 1783 when the Thirteen Colonies that became the United States gained independence from Great Britain

Civil Rights Movement: a time when people sought equal treatment for all genders and races

Constitution: the document that lays out the laws and plan of the United States

elected: to be chosen as a representative

Emancipation Proclamation: the freeing of all slaves within the confederacy on January 1, 1863

fierce: very strong and dangerous

Georgian style: a common architectural design between 1720 and 1840

immortality: the ability to live forever

independence: not ruled by another country

metamorphic: a type of rock that has changed in form from its original state

Muslim: people who follow the religion called Islam, or the submission to the will of Allah, the supreme being that Muslims worship

tyranny: unfair ruling or treatment

Index